U.S. Involvement in Vietnam

Essential Events

U.S. Involvement
IN Vietnam

BY MARTIN GITLIN

Content Consultant
Clarence R. Wyatt
Pottinger Professor of History
Centre College

ABDO
Publishing Company

CREDITS

Published by ABDO Publishing Company, 8000 West 78th Street,
Edina, Minnesota 55439. Copyright © 2010 by Abdo Consulting
Group, Inc. International copyrights reserved in all countries. No
part of this book may be reproduced in any form without written
permission from the publisher. The Essential Library™ is a
trademark and logo of ABDO Publishing Company.

Printed in the United States of America,
North Mankato, Minnesota
102009
012010

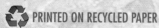 PRINTED ON RECYCLED PAPER

Editor: Mari Kesselring
Copy Editor: Paula Lewis
Interior Design and Production: Nicole Brecke
Cover Design: Nicole Brecke

Library of Congress Cataloging-in-Publication Data
Gitlin, Marty.
  U.S. involvement in Vietnam / Martin Gitlin.
    p. cm. — (Essential events)
  Includes bibliographical references and index.
  ISBN 978-1-60453-949-3
  1. Vietnam War, 1961-1975—United States—Juvenile literature. 2.
United States—History—1961-1969—Juvenile literature. 3. United
States—History—1969—Juvenile literature. I. Title.
  DS558.G575 2010
  959.704'3373—dc22
                                    2009031071

TABLE OF CONTENTS

South Vietnamese soldiers fought during a surprise Vietcong and North Vietnamese attack called the Tet Offensive.

Holiday Surprise

Peace and quiet was expected to fall pleasantly over war-torn Vietnam, at least for a while. It was late January 1968, and the combatants had agreed to halt the fighting in recognition of Tet, the Vietnamese New Year.

The break was to be a welcome one for soldiers and civilians alike. The conflict had been raging in the Southeast Asian nation since the end of World War II. And North Vietnam had been attempting to unify the country by imposing its communist government on South Vietnam since 1959.

More than 1 million people had already perished. This included nearly 20,000 Americans who had been sent halfway around the world to fight alongside the South Vietnamese and prevent a communist takeover. Among those who had died were South Vietnamese called Vietcong. They sympathized with the North Vietnamese and fought against the Americans. The war was getting bloodier by the day. So as Tet approached, many Americans and South Vietnamese were relieved. They assumed there would be no fighting during the holiday.

Ho Chi Minh's Poem

The signal to launch the Tet Offensive came in the form of a poem written by North Vietnamese President Ho Chi Minh. It was broadcast to his troops on January 29, 1968, from a radio station based in Hanoi, the capital of that country. The poem was read over the air as follows:

"This Spring far outshines the previous springs / Of victories throughout the land / Come happy tidings / Forward! / Total victory will be ours."[1]

By the next day, approximately 84,000 North Vietnamese and Vietcong troops had begun the attack.

They were wrong. The Vietcong had smuggled rifles underneath bunches of flowers into the South Vietnamese capital of Saigon. Some of the Vietcong's sympathizers in that city hid the enemy troops in their homes. On January 30, a group of 19 communist soldiers attacked the U.S. Embassy. Several U.S. military policemen began shooting back. One was Charles L. Daniel, who yelled frantically into his radio, "They're coming in! They're coming in! Help me! Help me!"[2]

There would be no help for Daniel, who was soon dead. Nor was there help for other Americans and South Vietnamese taken by surprise by what became known as the Tet Offensive. Vietcong and North Vietnamese troops also attacked dozens of other South Vietnamese cities, towns, villages, and military installations.

U.S. military leaders had anticipated a communist offensive around that time, but not one during the holiday, nor one so extensive. They believed the attack would be centered on Khe Sanh, a U.S. Marine base in the northwest corner of South Vietnam that had already been the focus of communist forces. But the Tet Offensive was centered nowhere. It was everywhere.

The Tet Offensive destroyed areas of Saigon.

Fortunately for the United States, the attack was also unsuccessful. Security was quickly reestablished at the U.S. Embassy. South Vietnamese and U.S. troops repelled attacks in Saigon and other areas of the country. The communist plan had been to create disorder. They hoped it would compel the South Vietnamese people to rise up against the United States and their own democratic government. But their plan had failed.

In early February, however, North Vietnam and its Vietcong allies tasted victory when they captured the coastal city of Hue. Their soldiers sought out and killed between 1,500 and 3,000 civilians who supported the South Vietnam government. However, by the end of the month, South Vietnamese and U.S. forces, also known as the Army of the Republic of Vietnam (ARVN), had taken back Hue. In the process, thousands of soldiers and civilians had died.

Years later, North Vietnamese commander General Tran Van Tra explained:

> *During Tet of 1968 we did not correctly evaluate the specific balance of forces between ourselves and the enemy. . . . [We set goals] that were beyond our actual strength. . . . We suffered large losses in material and men.*[3]

U.S. Public Opinion

Most experts agree that the Tet Offensive was a defeat for the North Vietnamese and Vietcong. Before this victory for U.S. forces, American support of the war and how it was being fought had been low. Now public opinion temporarily shifted. But soon, the U.S. public's support for the war continued its steady decline. Americans had been told by military leaders such as General William Westmoreland, commander of U.S. forces in Vietnam, that their country was on the verge of winning the conflict in Vietnam. But as the war continued and they watched in horror as events in Vietnam unfolded on their television screens, they became discouraged.

The Tet Offensive made some people realize that the enemy was still very much alive and the war was far from over. Reporter Jonathan Schell expressed his opinion of how the Tet Offensive affected the war:

> *The Vietnam War was a war for time, and in the war for time, what our foe had to do was not win battles but demonstrate that it could endure defeats. At Tet, the foe demonstrated its endurance beyond a shadow of a doubt, and in a way that the whole world could see and understand. It did this not by winning any battle but by launching the attack in the first place.*[4]

Televised Execution

During the Tet Offensive, Americans witnessed a shocking event on their televisions. South Vietnamese General Nguyen Ngoc Loan executed a suspected Vietcong officer on a Saigon street by shooting him in the head. With this action, Loan unwittingly played into the hands of the communists. His action supported the growing belief in the United States that the war was morally wrong.

Ordinary Americans were not the only people turning against the war. New U.S. Secretary of Defense Clark Clifford was also concerned. He concluded that military officials had no surefire plan to win in Vietnam. He offered his opinion to President Lyndon Johnson. Clifford argued that the war strategy needed to head in a different direction. General Westmoreland believed the new strategy should be heavier bombing in North Vietnam. He asked the president for 200,000 more U.S. troops, increasing the total to 700,000. But Johnson no longer believed in General Westmoreland, who was soon replaced by General Creighton Abrams.

Walter Cronkite

In September 1967, for the first time, the majority of Americans polled felt that U.S. involvement in Vietnam had been a mistake. By early 1968, only 26 percent of Americans polled approved of Johnson's handling of the war in Vietnam.

One journalist who turned against the war in early 1968 was iconic television anchorman Walter Cronkite. It had been said that U.S. public opinion generally mirrored that of the respected and trusted Cronkite. On his return from a trip to Vietnam in late February, Cronkite gave his opinion that the best the United States could hope for was a stalemate and thousands more dead. He added that the only honorable solution was negotiating for peace. That was the last thing President Johnson wanted to hear. Since Johnson had first sent combat troops to Vietnam in early 1965, the number of U.S. soldiers fighting the war had risen to 500,000.

When Cronkite spoke out against the war, Johnson reportedly said, "If I've lost Cronkite, I've lost Middle America."[5] He was right.

Meanwhile, the antiwar movement in the United States intensified. Millions protested against the war. They held signs and chanted slogans. One of the chants addressed the president, Lyndon Baines Johnson, by his initials: "Hey, hey LBJ, how many kids did you kill today?"

Such criticism tormented Johnson, who knew his decision to continue U.S. involvement was costing thousands of lives. He knew the debate over the war was tearing the country apart. But he had made a commitment to South Vietnam to keep it noncommunist. He also believed that it was his duty to prevent communism from spreading anywhere in the world. Johnson also knew that his own political career was at stake. His public opinion ratings would decrease even more if he allowed South Vietnam to fall to communism.

Pressure to end the war came not only from protesters but also from Johnson's own Democratic Party. In the first stage of the 1968 election, antiwar candidate Eugene McCarthy nearly defeated Johnson in the New Hampshire primary. That motivated the highly popular politician Robert Kennedy, who also called for an end to U.S. involvement in Vietnam, to enter the campaign.

Americans shocked by the Tet Offensive were in for another surprise when Johnson addressed them via television on March 31, 1968. He announced he was going to reduce the bombing of North Vietnam and send only a token number of additional troops into the war. Then a somber Johnson dropped the bombshell: he was withdrawing from the presidential race. Johnson could not justify waging an election campaign and a war at the same time. A new president would have to deal with the conflict—one in which, by that time, most Americans wished their country had never gotten involved. ⌐

On March 31, 1968, President Johnson announced that he would not run for another term as president.

Ho Chi Minh

WAR ON THE HORIZON

One would have found it hard to believe during the Vietnam War that Ho Chi Minh, the president of North Vietnam, had been an ally of the United States during World War II. He had led the communist Vietminh party. The

Vietminh had worked with the United States to defeat Japan. Minh, who took control of the northern section of Vietnam soon after the end of World War II, hoped to maintain that friendship.

The problem for the U.S. government was that Minh was a communist. The United States simply did not make friends with communists. The communist economic and political system was seen as a threat to democracy and capitalism. Following World War II, the United States made halting the spread of communism a primary goal.

By 1950, two of the three major military and political powers in the world had been converted to communism. Both the Soviet Union and China supported Ho Chi Minh and his Vietminh party in their fight against the French. Vietnam was a colony of France. Minh and his Vietminh were seeking independence for the Vietnamese people.

Meanwhile, the United States was showing that it was serious about stopping the advance of communism. President Harry Truman sent forces

Vietnam Freed from Colonial Rule

The final defeat of France in its fight to maintain control over Vietnam occurred in the town of Dien Bien Phu. In March 1954, the Vietminh surrounded 12,000 French troops. France called upon the United States to help, but Eisenhower and the U.S. Congress were not about to send troops to Asia so soon after the end of the Korean War. After two months, the French surrendered. Their colonial rule of Vietnam, which had started in 1883, was over.

to Korea after communist North Korea invaded noncommunist South Korea in 1950. This was the beginning of the Korean War. China, which had become a communist country only a year earlier, fought on the side of the North Koreans. The United States and other nations that backed South Korea stemmed the tide of communism by preventing North Korea from unifying the two countries under a communist flag. Soon after that task was completed, the United States decided it must turn its attention to Vietnam. In 1954,

What Is Communism?

Communism is a system in which the government plans and controls the economy and the equal sharing of goods and services among all the people. The purpose is to create a classless society in which there are neither rich nor poor people.

The only communist country in the world before 1945 was the Soviet Union. After its triumph in World War II, the Soviet Union imposed communism upon a number of Eastern European nations, such as East Germany and Poland. Other countries, such as China and Cuba, also adopted communism in later years.

The economic and political system has not, however, improved the lives of the people who lived under it. The failure of communism has given way to democracy in much of Eastern Europe. Even the countries of the former Soviet Union no longer practice communism.

Communist regimes have been criticized for suspending liberties such as freedom of speech and freedom of the press. They have not held open elections. They have also been known to deal ruthlessly with those who have dared to criticize their governments. In the United States and other democratic countries, citizens are generally free to say or write whatever they want about those in power.

the Vietminh ousted the French. It was feared that Ho Chi Minh would then attempt to spread communism throughout Vietnam.

TURNING TO VIETNAM

Those fears were justified. China and the Soviet Union had been steadily supplying the Vietminh with military equipment and advisers since 1950. Dwight Eisenhower, who was elected U.S. president in 1952, was a proponent of the domino theory. This was the belief that once China and Russia helped establish communism in one Asian country, the rest of the nations would fall to communism one by one—like dominoes.

Following the French defeat, representatives from the United States, the Soviet Union, and several other countries met in Switzerland to debate the future of Vietnam. In an agreement called the Geneva Accords, it was decided to grant the nation its complete independence and temporarily divide it into North Vietnam, led by Ho Chi Minh and the Vietminh, and South Vietnam.

The division was set to last for no more than two years. Within that period, elections would be held to decide the leader of a united Vietnam. The United

South Vietnamese Prime Minister Ngo Dinh Diem,
second from the right, with his family

States was against this decision, fearing that Minh
was popular enough to win the election and establish
communism in all of Vietnam.

By 1955, South Vietnam was being led by Prime
Minister Ngo Dinh Diem. He proved to be a brutal
dictator. Diem dealt ruthlessly with his political
opponents. He refused to hold the elections that
had been called for in Switzerland. He placed his

relatives in high-profile government jobs. He also stole land from those who practiced the Buddhist religion and gave it to Catholics.

In North Vietnam, Minh was popular. He wanted to hold the elections called for in the Geneva Accords. But the United States knew this would put Minh and communism in power. So the United States supported Diem, who vowed to thwart a communist takeover. The U.S. government was criticized for backing a corrupt leader simply because of his stand against communism, but President Eisenhower held his position. In a speech justifying the policy of giving aid to South Vietnam, he even praised Diem for defending freedom.

Seeking Change in South Vietnam

The hatred of Diem's rule caused many South Vietnamese to organize the National Liberation Front (NLF), an antigovernment organization. They promoted the

Ho Chi Minh

Born in Vietnam in 1890, Ho Chi Minh traveled all over the world. He worked in London during World War I. After that he moved to Paris and helped establish the French Communist Party shortly after Russia turned to communism in 1917 and became the Soviet Union.

From that point on, Minh yearned to bring communism to his native Vietnam. He hoped to use communism to free Vietnam from its French rulers.

overthrow of Diem's government and an end to U.S. involvement in their country. They called for the reunification of Vietnam. Though Diem and his U.S. allies claimed that communists who had infiltrated from North Vietnam created the NLF, others believed it represented a genuine popular uprising against Diem. Many in the NLF joined the People's Liberation Armed Forces. Also known as the Vietcong, this military force was no less brutal than Diem and his army. The Vietcong murdered thousands of Diem supporters.

In North Vietnam, Ho Chi Minh ordered thousands of peasant landowners killed for allegedly failing to follow communist rules. The North Vietnamese also provided economic and military support to the Vietcong. This helped make the Vietcong powerful enough to run some local governments in South Vietnam.

The United States Reacts

When John F. Kennedy assumed the presidency in 1961, he vowed to keep communism from spreading. Kennedy did not want to send U.S. troops into Vietnam. However, he did increase aid to South Vietnam and dispatch thousands of military advisers to help fight what was becoming a greater North Vietnamese threat.

Diem's policies also proved to be upsetting stability in South Vietnam. His violent repression of his people caused them to rebel during the summer of 1963. In November of that year, the South Vietnamese military staged an overthrow of the government. During the overthrow, Diem was assassinated.

Kennedy now believed something had to be done. The United States had been providing economic and military aid for several years, but South Vietnam was still in chaos. Kennedy was in the process of rethinking his strategy when he was assassinated in November 1963. The responsibility of steering U.S. policy in Vietnam would be heaped upon the shoulders of Lyndon Johnson.

President Johnson increased the number of U.S. military advisers, who trained and advised South Vietnamese military personnel, in South Vietnam from 16,000

Thich Quang Duc's Suicide

A few Buddhists who protested their treatment by the South Vietnamese government in the early 1960s did so quite dramatically. They burned themselves to death.

Buddhist monk Thich Quang Duc performed the most famous suicide. In the late spring of 1963, he doused himself with gasoline and set himself on fire. The act was caught by television cameras, which showed the incident around the world, horrifying millions.

to 23,000. But Johnson held back on sending ground troops. Johnson's basic plan was to continue Kennedy's policies and remain cautious. But after an event on August 2, 1964, called the Gulf of Tonkin Incident, Johnson felt he had to take further action. On this day, a North Vietnamese ship in the Gulf of Tonkin reportedly fired upon a patrolling U.S. warship, the USS *Maddox*. Two days later, the USS *C. Turner Joy* and *Maddox* crews claimed they were under attack. In the end, though, no Americans were injured in either incident.

Some critics believe the second attack was fabricated, or at least exaggerated, to give Johnson and the U.S. Congress an excuse to approve the deployment of ground troops in Vietnam. Regardless, on August 7, Congress passed the Gulf of Tonkin Resolution. This stated that the president could take any steps he deemed necessary to prevent further aggression by North Vietnam. Johnson had a green light. And the only war the United States has ever lost was about to begin.

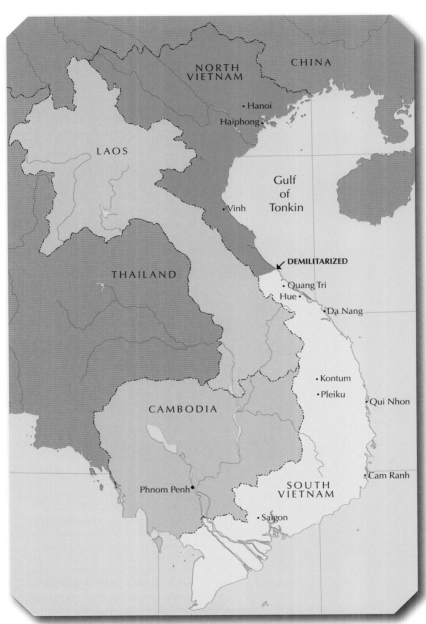

CHINA

NORTH
VIETNAM

LAOS

• Hanoi

Haiphong •

Gulf
of
Tonkin

• Vinh

THAILAND

➤ DEMILITARIZED

• Quang Tri
Hue •

• Da Nang

• Kontum
• Pleiku

• Qui Nhon

CAMBODIA

• Cam Ranh

SOUTH
VIETNAM

Phnom Penh •

• Saigon

Vietnam was divided into North Vietnam and South Vietnam in 1954.

*President Johnson first authorized air attacks
against the North Vietnamese.*

THE GREEN LIGHT

There were no second thoughts on August 7,
1964, when the U.S. House of
Representatives and the Senate voted on the Gulf of
Tonkin Resolution. The House of Representatives
passed it unanimously. The Senate vote was an

overwhelming 88–2 in favor of it. Most people in the country felt that it was necessary to take action in Vietnam.

Even with the backing of Congress, Johnson hoped to avoid a ground war involving the United States. He did not want to rush American men into battle on the eve of the 1964 presidential election. His restraint proved wise, particularly because he was running against Republican Barry Goldwater. Many believed Goldwater would rush into war if elected. Johnson defeated Goldwater by a landslide.

But any hope Johnson had that time would end the chaos in South Vietnam was soon dashed. Military leaders estimated that the Vietcong controlled more than half the country. In one incident, the Vietcong attacked a U.S. air base, killing four Americans. The North Vietnamese bombed a private home for U.S. officers on Christmas Eve in 1964, killing 2 and wounding 98.

Such tragedies, however, did not convince Johnson to escalate U.S. involvement in Vietnam. The final straw was the continuing collapse of the South Vietnamese government. Its army was facing defeat by the Vietcong, which was now being supplemented by the North Vietnamese

Army (NVA). Further aggression by the Vietcong, including an attack on U.S. bases in early February 1965, particularly angered the president. He said:

We have kept our guns over the mantel and our shells in the cupboard for a long time now. I can't ask American soldiers out there to continue to fight with one hand tied behind their backs.[1]

No Tunnel Vision

One creative strategy the Vietcong and North Vietnamese used during the war was to build a series of underground tunnels in South Vietnam that could serve as military bases. The tunnels had several uses. They provided a place to hide or escape from the enemy. They also served as areas in which to train soldiers as well as passageways between aboveground facilities.

The tunnels were intricate. They contained rooms in which the Vietcong and North Vietnamese could manufacture and store weapons. They featured kitchens, sleeping areas, and first-aid stations. Smoke from the kitchen stoves was directed sideways, which allowed the tunnel dwellers to keep their location a secret from the Americans and the ARVN.

Some of the bases were quite expansive. One located just 20 miles (32.1 km) from the capital city of Saigon featured nearly 75 miles (120.7 km) of underground tunnels. During and after the war, U.S. soldiers spoke often about their frustration in trying to flush out an enemy that was using such tunnels so cleverly.

Military Action

Johnson had seen enough. He ordered a program of sustained bombing of North Vietnam with the code name Operation Rolling Thunder. But after two months of air attacks, military advisers suggested to Johnson that they were not damaging the

North Vietnamese war effort. Rolling Thunder continued to pound away at military and industrial targets. It also targeted the Ho Chi Minh Trail, which was used to transport weapons and soldiers from North Vietnam to the Vietcong in the south.

Finally, Johnson was convinced that air attacks alone were not the answer. In early March 1965, he sent U.S. Marines to South Vietnam to guard air bases. By the summer of 1965, more than 70,000 U.S. soldiers had joined the battle. These ground troops were no longer told to merely defend U.S. air bases. They were to hunt down and kill the Vietcong.

Johnson versus Goldwater

Johnson received a boost during the 1964 presidential campaign when opponent Barry Goldwater came out in favor of directly attacking North Vietnam. Though others shared that view, most Americans considered that approach reckless and dangerous. Johnson's moderate stance on Vietnam helped him easily win the election.

The success of the combat mission required stability in South Vietnam. Johnson hoped that would be achieved by General Nguyen Van Thieu and Air Marshal Nguyen Cao Ky, who formed a new government. But the two South Vietnamese military leaders did not appear to be committed to the cause. U.S. General Westmoreland lamented

General Westmoreland asked for more troops in 1965.

that South Vietnamese soldiers were deserting the
army in droves. He asked for 200,000 more U.S.
troops by the end of the year. Johnson and the
nation wondered when the escalation would end.
Presidential aide Jack Valenti recalled Johnson asking
Westmoreland, "What happens if in two, three, four
years you ask me for 500,000 men?"[2] Johnson
might not have agreed to send 175,000 men to

Vietnam by the end of 1965 if he had known those fears would come true.

BIRTH OF THE ANTIWAR MOVEMENT

The decision to send a fighting force to Vietnam not only committed the United States to a prolonged war in Vietnam, but it gave rise to the protest movement. In May 1965, several universities hosted "teach-ins," which included informal antiwar speeches and rallies. By the end of the year, hundreds of demonstrations against U.S. involvement in Vietnam had taken place in the United States and around the world. Antiwar sentiment, however, was comparatively small at this point. The vast majority of Americans supported Johnson's decision to send in ground troops. Many feared that the withdrawal of U.S. forces would result in a communist takeover throughout Southeast Asia.

Kennedy's View on Vietnam

Some have speculated that President Kennedy would not have sent U.S. ground troops into battle. That theory is given weight by his statements about Vietnam in September 1963, just two months before he was killed. He said, "In the final analysis, it is their war. They are the ones who have to win it or lose it. We can help them, we can give them equipment, we can send our men out there as [advisers], but they have to win it."[3]

Kennedy did go on to say, however, that Vietnam should not be abandoned. One can only wonder what he would have done had he been faced with the collapse of South Vietnam.

First Fighting Forces

The first fighting forces that arrived in Vietnam believed the enemy would be defeated quickly. After all, the United States had never lost a war. It was not about to lose against North Vietnam, which was anything but a world power. Among those marines confident that they would make fast work of the enemy was Lieutenant Philip Caputo. He later wrote about his feelings upon entering the battlefields of Vietnam:

> [When] we marched into the rice paddies on that damp March afternoon we carried, along with our packs and rifles, the implicit conviction that the [Vietcong] would be quickly beaten.[4]

"Hawks" and "Doves"

Two particular species of birds received plenty of attention in the United States during the Vietnam War. People who supported U.S. involvement in Vietnam were called "hawks." Those who did not were called "doves."

But Caputo and his fellow soldiers were in for a rude awakening. War conditions in Vietnam were unlike any the United States had experienced. There was no front line, as in World War II, where enemies traditionally do battle. U.S. soldiers in Vietnam were forced to seek out the enemy, who could be hiding anywhere in the country's dense jungles. So U.S. soldiers set out on search-and-destroy missions to find the elusive North Vietnamese and Vietcong. Many U.S. soldiers were killed by an enemy they never saw.

An occasional battle did arise. One such battle was in November 1965, shortly after the first significant wave of U.S. troops arrived in Vietnam. The NVA launched an attack at the Ia Drang Valley that lasted two days. Fierce fights ensued that sometimes required hand-to-hand combat. By the time the guns stopped firing, more than 3,000 North Vietnamese and 300 Americans lay dead. Though the NVA was stymied, U.S. troops discovered that there were many more NVA soldiers in South Vietnam than they had anticipated. U.S. soldiers also began to realize that this was not going to be an easy war. Battalion commander Hal Moore remembered it well. He said:

> Among my sergeants, there were . . . men who had parachuted
> into Normandy [during the invasion of Europe in World

Air Cavalry

A new kind of U.S. combat unit, the Air Cavalry, was unveiled in the Battle of the Ia Drang Valley. The force had been created as part of President Kennedy's plan to improve the capacity of the U.S. military to wage a ground war. It used helicopters to give ground combat units greater mobility. The Air Cavalry first arrived in Vietnam in July 1965 during President Johnson's escalation of U.S. involvement in the war.

War II] and had survived the war in Korea—and those old veterans were shocked by the savagery and hellish noise of this battle. Choking clouds of smoke and dust obscured the killing ground. We were dry-mouthed and [overcome] with fear, and still the enemy came on in waves.[5]

It was just the beginning. Those who believed that the Americans, with their superior technology, could overwhelm the NVA and Vietcong with sheer firepower soon changed their point of view. ⌐

*U.S. soldiers forged ahead after a U.S. Air Force bombing raid
in Ia Drang Valley on November 16, 1965.*

Antiwar protesters marched in Philadelphia in March 1966.

GETTING IN DEEPER
AND DEEPER

ome Americans who fought in Vietnam
or supported U.S. involvement there
believed that the antiwar movement played into
the hands of the North Vietnamese and Vietcong.
These Americans claimed that the knowledge that

millions in the United States were protesting the war gave comfort to the enemy. On the other side, the antiwar advocates believed it was their right and duty as Americans to protest what they considered to be a dangerous, immoral, or ill-conceived policy. They emphasized that they were trying to save lives by bringing U.S. soldiers home. The debate that raged in the 1960s continues today. However, there is little doubt that the North Vietnamese and Vietcong proved to be far more motivated fighters than the ARVN.

North Vietnamese leader Ho Chi Minh believed that his communist cause was greatly served by the protest movement in the United States—even as early as 1965. During a speech to the National Assembly of the Democratic Republic of Vietnam, he expressed pity for those U.S. servicemen who had died. He also praised those who had voiced antiwar sentiment:

> The American people have been [fooled] by the propaganda of their government, which has [stolen] from them billions of dollars to throw into the crater of war. Thousands of American youths—their sons and brothers—have met a tragic death or have been pitifully wounded on the Vietnamese battlefields thousands of miles from the United States.

At present, many mass organizations and individuals in the United States are demanding that their government at once stop this unjust war and withdraw U.S. troops from South Vietnam. Our people are resolved to drive away . . . our sworn enemy. But we always express our friendship with the progressive American people.[1]

Those "progressive American people" grew more alarmed as a greater number of U.S. servicemen were sent into combat. Westmoreland, who had asked for 200,000 additional troops in 1965, renewed that request in late 1966. Johnson provided 200,000 more soldiers, which pushed the total number of U.S. forces in Vietnam to nearly 400,000.

Weather in Vietnam

If the terrain was not difficult enough, the weather presented more problems for U.S. soldiers in Vietnam. The monsoon winds struck throughout the rainy season, resulting in massive torrents of rain. During the dry season, the scorching heat made it unbearably uncomfortable for soldiers trudging around in uniforms and 70 pounds (32 kg) of equipment and ammunition.

A Foreign Experience

Those who hoped an increased presence in Vietnam would result in quick victory would be disappointed. Westmoreland limited the tour of duty for each soldier to one year. This meant that thousands of troops unfamiliar with fighting in Vietnam were learning the ropes at all times.

Many have argued that it took at least one year for U.S. combat troops to understand how to fight in such an unusual and difficult environment. By the time that year was up, the troops were sent home.

The terrain in Vietnam was not favorable to fighting. The southern area of South Vietnam was laden with watery rice fields, swampland, and forests. North of Saigon, U.S. soldiers encountered sparsely populated forests, rugged mountain peaks, and waterfalls. The enemy could be hiding anywhere. Conditions were made more perilous by booby traps and mines planted by the enemy. Thousands

The Deadly Spray

Flushing out the Vietcong hiding in South Vietnamese jungles became a priority for the U.S. military early in the war. The problem became so acute in 1962 that the United States began spraying the jungles with a chemical that destroyed the plant life the enemy used for cover. The substance was colorless, but it was named Agent Orange for the orange stripe painted on its storage containers.

An estimated 20 million gallons (75.7 million l) of Agent Orange were sent streaming into the jungles for nearly a decade during the war. Afterward, thousands of South Vietnamese and U.S. veterans began developing cancer, skin rashes, and liver disease that they blamed on exposure to the chemical.

Initially, the Department of Veterans Affairs denied claims related to Agent Orange exposure. In 1979, Vietnam veterans filed a class-action lawsuit against a large group of chemical companies that had been involved in the manufacture of Agent Orange, but the case never went to court. Instead, a settlement was reached in which the companies paid $180 million in damages.

U.S. soldiers were forced to wade through Vietnam's marshlands.

of U.S. soldiers were killed or injured by mines that exploded as they took a fateful step on the wrong spot.

Among the civilian population, it was difficult for U.S. soldiers to tell a friend from an enemy. Most villagers did not care about democracy or communism. They simply yearned to live in peace. They viewed U.S. troops with anger and suspicion. Other South Vietnamese citizens were working, either willingly or by force, with the Vietcong, but many U.S. soldiers did not find that out until it was too late.

VICTORIES AND DEFEATS

The United States achieved a series of military victories in 1966. However, these successes did not bring them any closer to overall victory. The First Infantry Division drove the Vietcong into the neighboring country of Cambodia in June. This prevented an anticipated attack on Saigon. Meanwhile, the First Cavalry Division defeated three enemy regiments, capturing dozens of Vietcong suspects and tons of weaponry.

Farther north in March 1966, the First Marine Division worked with the South Vietnamese forces against the NVA. In one battle, the North Vietnamese lost one-third of its force but killed 98 Americans. In July 1966, a U.S. Marine battalion staved off an attack by 1,000 NVA soldiers. The battle intensified as 8,000 marines and 3,000 South Vietnamese engaged 12,000 enemy troops. The result was a defeat for the North Vietnamese, who lost 800 men.

Later battles proved that large numbers of men and advanced

Early Casualties

On average, 500 Americans were killed each month in Vietnam by the end of 1966. As that year came to an end, more than 5,000 U.S. soldiers had died. That total alarmed Americans. But it would prove to be less than 10 percent of all U.S. combat deaths suffered in Vietnam by the end of the war in 1973.

technology did not translate into victory. They also showed that despite huge losses, the enemy continually rebuilt its forces with fresh troops. A typical mission occurred late in 1966. The U.S. troops embarked on a search-and-destroy sweep through the jungles of enemy strongholds. Several weeks produced little contact with the Vietcong. But as the 196th Light Infantry Brigade moved closer to the Cambodian border, the enemy was waiting. The result was victory for the U.S. troops. The United States suffered many casualties in the process. Still, the success of that operation convinced U.S. military leaders that such search-and-destroy missions would lead to success in Vietnam. That theory would be put to the test in 1967.

So would the United States' commitment to the war. Thousands of miles away, the protests against a U.S. presence in Vietnam were escalating. The most dedicated in the antiwar movement were vowing to "bring the war home" through violent protests. The battle in Vietnam had been raging for years, but the battle in the United States was just ramping up.

U.S. marines question a 12-year-old boy about Vietcong hideouts.

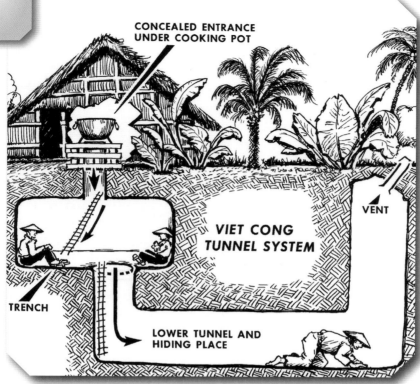

CONCEALED ENTRANCE
UNDER COOKING POT

VENT

VIET CONG
TUNNEL SYSTEM

TRENCH

LOWER TUNNEL AND
HIDING PLACE

The Vietcong used tunnels as hideouts and for secret storage.

CONFLICT ON
THE HOME FRONT

y 1967, the Vietcong had established a major base northwest of Saigon. This area was a critical stronghold known as the Iron Triangle. There, local villagers, either through sympathy or force, aided the Vietcong with food and shelter. In 1967, U.S. soldiers attempted to break up the base in a massive search-and-destroy mission. The mission was called Operation Cedar Falls.

The enemy used an intricate underground tunnel network to store food and ammunition. During the 19-day sweep, the U.S soldiers unearthed the tunnels and seized the area's Vietcong headquarters. Although approximately 750 Vietcong perished, the vast majority of enemy soldiers escaped toward Cambodia. In Cambodia, supply lines continued to feed and arm them.

The frustrated U.S. and South Vietnamese forces were ordered to track down the Vietcong. The U.S. and South Vietnamese soldiers evacuated and destroyed nearby villages where the Vietcong might be hiding, dressed as civilians. The practice would become familiar to

Counterdemonstrations

Not all demonstrations motivated by U.S. involvement in Vietnam were carried out by antiwar protesters. Thousands of people marched and demonstrated in support of President Johnson's policies. Many of those who protested against the protesters held what were known as "counterdemonstrations." Those who favored continuing the war often held demonstrations near the antiwar protests. At times, this resulted in heated arguments and even violent clashes.

U.S. soldiers who could not distinguish between South Vietnamese peasants and Vietcong dressed as civilians. It would also become a frightening prospect for South Vietnamese citizens. Many were forced to watch their homes burn to the ground. Many innocent people were killed during the process.

A SENSE OF CHAOS

Reports of brutality on both sides and the increasing number of U.S. soldiers returning home in body bags angered millions of Americans. Finally, the antiwar movement exploded in 1967. On October 21, approximately 50,000 protesters marched to the Pentagon in Washington DC, the heart of the U.S. military. An estimated 2,500 U.S. Army troops stood in front of the building to meet them. Some of those who sought peace in Vietnam placed flowers in the barrels of the soldiers' bayoneted rifles. But nearly 700 protesters were arrested when the march turned violent. Protester Marcus Raskin recalled, "People became frightened. They began running every which way. At that moment, it turned into something else. A sense of chaos took over."[1]

*Military police and protesters conflicted during
the 1967 protest at the Pentagon.*

That sense of chaos seemed to grip the country
for the next two years. Antiwar protests became
particularly destructive on college campuses. A
majority of students turned against U.S. involvement
in the war, not just on moral grounds, but for
personal reasons. They became horrified when
their friends or family members died in Vietnam
or returned home wounded. Those students feared
they could be next. American men often did not
have a choice whether to become soldiers. Many were
selected to fight in Vietnam through a system called
the draft. Many people were alarmed when U.S.

troop levels reached nearly 500,000 by December 1967 with no end in sight. And while Americans were dying in record numbers in South Vietnam, Ho Chi Minh and his government were no closer to the bargaining table.

By the end of 1967, U.S. planes had dropped 864,000 tons (783,816 tonnes) of bombs on North Vietnam. They nearly destroyed entire villages in the process. The lack of success in weakening the North Vietnamese economy and morale discouraged those running the

---

The Chosen Ones

All American men were required to register with the Selective Service agency when they reached the age of 18. This meant that they could be drafted to fight in the war. That agency categorized all of those young men by eligibility. Most were slotted into 1-A, which meant they were eligible for military service. Those classified at 4-F were not eligible due to mental or physical health problems.

Draft calls were issued every month. If a man received a draft call, he was required by law to report for military service. The number of those drafted into the service depended upon the needs of the nation. At the height of the war, approximately 125,000 men were drafted on a monthly basis.

The draft was criticized for its perceived unfairness. Those in college received a deferment, which allowed them to delay their service in Vietnam. That resulted in poorer people, who could not afford college, being sent in higher numbers to fight in the war. African Americans and other minority members, as well as rural whites, were predominantly dispatched to Vietnam. Many who did not believe in the U.S. war policy simply refused to register or faked medical conditions in an attempt to be classified as 4-F. Thousands of others who were drafted fled to Canada to avoid fighting in Vietnam.

war. Despite the pummeling from the skies, the North Vietnamese managed to send in three times more supplies to the NVA and Vietcong in South Vietnam than they had before the bombing began.

A Strategy Gone Wrong

Meanwhile, General Westmoreland's tactic of overwhelming the enemy with numbers and advanced weaponry was not working either. The U.S. Defense Department later admitted that Westmoreland exaggerated the number of enemy soldiers killed by at least 30 percent. It had been estimated that 220,000 NVA and Vietcong troops had perished since the United States sent ground troops to Vietnam. Yet by the end of 1967, approximately 350,000 communist troops were fighting the war. And every year, 200,000 North Vietnamese boys reached the age in

"Fragging"

One unfortunate consequence of the soldiers' disillusionment with the war was that some used violence against their superior officers. A few even attempted to or succeeded in killing superiors they considered too strict or too likely to send them into harm's way.

Several hundred U.S. officers were victims of murder or attempted murder in Vietnam. The practice became known as "fragging" from the name of the weapon often used to carry out these murders—the fragmentation grenade. Instances of fragging increased as the war dragged on.

which they could be enlisted in the army.

In addition, the United States was losing the battle to win over the South Vietnamese. Most of the South Vietnamese simply wanted peace—no matter what political and economic system they lived under. More and more befriended the North Vietnamese and Vietcong as time marched on. During one press conference, a reporter confronted a briefing officer from the U.S. military with a question about that very problem. The reporter asked,

> *It appears you [have] leveled virtually every village and hamlet, killed or driven more than 50,000 peasants off the land with your firepower. My question is, how do you intend to go about winning the hearts and minds of these people? The briefing officer replied, "I'm afraid you'll have to take that up with Civic Affairs. But it's a real good question."[2]*

Doctor Benjamin Spock

One influential American who expressed antiwar sentiment was Benjamin Spock. A pediatrician, Spock had published a book in 1946 called *Baby and Child Care* that was a guide for millions of U.S. parents on how to raise their children. His message was that parents should give their kids plenty of freedom and affection.

In 1967, Spock and several others published a document titled "A Call to Resist Illegitimate Authority," in which they expressed outrage over the killing in Vietnam. Spock felt a kinship with the generation of American soldiers and was upset that so many of them were dying.

It was a good question for U.S. leaders as well, but not all of them were answering it the same way. Military leaders pushed to intensify the bombing of North Vietnam. They approved of Westmoreland's request to send 200,000 additional troops. On the other hand, an increasing number of national leaders were joining the antiwar ranks. They called for a complete withdrawal from Vietnam.

The only voice that truly counted was that of President Johnson. And despite his growing concern about his war policy, he spoke to Congress about his commitment to U.S. involvement in Vietnam. As 1968 approached, he said, "We are not going to yield. We are not going to shimmy. We are going to wind up with a peace with honor which all Americans seek."[3]

The communists had other ideas, which they were about to unveil in the

Predicted Success in 1968

Just before the Tet Offensive in January 1968, General Westmoreland offered a positive outlook for U.S. involvement in Vietnam. He wrote, "During 1967, the enemy lost control of large sectors of the population. . . . In many areas the enemy has been driven away from the population centers; in others he has been compelled to disperse and evade contact, thus [losing] much of his potential. . . . The friendly picture gives rise to optimism for increased successes in 1968."[4]

Tet Offensive. Soon 1967 would turn into 1968, one of the most volatile years in U.S. history. ⌐

As more men were wounded and killed in battle,
U.S. support for the war decreased.

The village of My Lai several months after the My Lai Massacre

THE WORLD
IS WATCHING

What many believe to be the most dishonorable incident in U.S. military history occurred on March 16, 1968. A platoon, under the command of Army Lieutenant William Calley, was ordered to destroy the small South

Vietnamese village of My Lai and all its inhabitants. The civilians in the village were suspected of aiding the Vietcong. U.S. soldiers anticipated battle with the Vietcong, but when the soldiers arrived, they saw no trace of the Vietcong. They saw only villagers going about their daily business. But the soldiers were given their orders. They rounded up more than 500 My Lai men, women, and children—many of them begging to be spared—and shot them.

Afterward, the U.S. Army attempted to keep the massacre a secret, but the story leaked out in 1969. Calley was convicted of first-degree murder and given life in prison in 1971. However, his sentence was quickly reduced to house arrest in which he was guarded in his own home. In 1974, he was freed.

The My Lai incident brought about furious debate in the United States. For many people, the incident showed a breakdown in the discipline and leadership that military training is meant to instill. Others saw the incident as evidence that such

The Wounded

Among the unsung U.S. heroes in Vietnam were the medical personnel who tended to the thousands of wounded soldiers. Soldiers were not only struck by bullets, but they also fell victim to land mines and other booby traps. The wounded first received treatment for their injuries in the field. They were transported to field hospitals by medical evacuation helicopters to receive additional treatment. Doctors and nurses performed surgeries or other procedures in an attempt to save a limb or even a life.

training reduces the value of human life and makes it easier for soldiers to kill.

But in 1968, violence and killing were not limited to Vietnam. On April 4, civil rights leader and Nobel Peace Prize winner Martin Luther King Jr. was assassinated. The nation grieved. King's murder sparked rioting among blacks throughout U.S. inner cities that resulted in more deaths. Two months later, Robert Kennedy was shot and killed. Kennedy, who was brother to assassinated U.S. President John F. Kennedy, had just won the California primary on an antiwar platform. He appeared well on his way to the Democratic nomination when a gunman ended his life.

This left the antiwar movement with no presidential

Fooling the Public

It has been said that honesty is the best policy, but it was not always the policy used by the U.S. military during the Vietnam War. The truth about the number of enemy troops killed was often exaggerated in an attempt to convince the U.S. public and leaders that the war was being won.

General Westmoreland was greatly criticized after the war for both encouraging and claiming false body counts. Westmoreland believed that the number of enemy casualties showed how successful the U.S. Army was in the war. Because of this, Westmoreland and his staff often used dead Vietnamese civilians, including women and children, in their counts. Other military leaders would also inflate their counts, hoping to increase their perceived success in the war. By 1968, this system had been widely discredited. It was abandoned after Westmoreland left his position in 1968.

candidates. It was clear that the Democratic Vice President Hubert Humphrey and Republican Richard Nixon would run for president. They both favored continued U.S. involvement in Vietnam. This angered and frustrated those who wanted to end the conflict. Writer Jack Newfield expressed his opinion:

> We had already glimpsed the most compassionate leaders our nation could produce, and they had all been assassinated. And from this time forward, things would get worse. Our best political leaders were part of memory now, not hope.[1]

Battle in the Windy City

A new battle was brewing—and it was not in Vietnam. It was in Chicago, where the Democrats held their convention to officially announce Humphrey as their presidential candidate. This meant President Johnson's war platform would be continued. When thousands of enraged antiwar protesters converged on the city, what many have described as a police riot resulted.

While millions of Americans watched on television, an estimated 18,000 Chicago police and Illinois National Guardsmen surged into the

*A police riot erupted in Chicago during
the 1968 Democratic National Convention.*

crowd. They beat protesters and even some innocent
bystanders with clubs. They arrested hundreds. Many
protesters began chanting, "The whole world is
watching! The whole world is watching!"

The turbulence in Chicago gave Nixon an edge in
U.S. public opinion. Though Nixon was also against
withdrawing forces from Vietnam, he did promise an
honorable end to the war. Humphrey, however, had

supported Johnson's position on the war. Nixon won
a close election in November.

THE FIGHT CONTINUES

The war, however, was far from over. The
communists had attacked throughout South
Vietnam. Just before the Tet Offensive, they had
put the U.S. combat base Khe Sanh, near the
North Vietnamese border, under siege, trapping
nearly 6,000 marines. The U.S. soldiers prevented
a takeover of their base, but they could not push
back the enemy. Then, in February and March
1968, U.S. warplanes dropped 100,000 tons
(90,719 tonnes) of bombs on the NVA. This helped
break the siege, but 200 marines were killed during
the 77-day ordeal. A decision was made to shut down
the combat base. It was deemed too close to the
North Vietnamese border and far too vulnerable to
attack.

The Tet Offensive was not the end of communist
aggression in South Vietnam. Communist forces
began another offensive throughout the country in
May despite the beginning of peace talks in Paris
between the United States and North Vietnam.
Demands by both sides doomed the discussions

As the war marched on, more young Americans took steps to avoid going to Vietnam. One of the most dramatic displays of refusal to fight in the war was the burning of draft cards. During the march on the Pentagon in October 1967, hundreds of young men pulled out matches or lighters and ceremoniously torched their draft cards.

to failure. The Americans insisted that the NVA withdraw from South Vietnam. The North Vietnamese wanted the NLF to be included in a peacetime South Vietnamese government.

In one of Johnson's last major decisions about the war, Rolling Thunder was halted. The bombing of North Vietnam was ended on November 1. It was an attempt to bring that country back to the stalled Paris peace talks. But North Vietnam's break from bombing would not last.

Nixon became president in January 1969. While he slowly withdrew U.S. troops, he increased the bombing of North Vietnam. Now it was up to the new president to try to heal the wounds and bring together a deeply divided nation.

Ken Love burned his draft card in protest of the war.

Many soldiers were wounded or killed while they tried to capture Dong Ap Bia.

INCHING OUT

s Richard Nixon was sworn in as president of the United States on January 20, 1969, more Americans were fighting and dying in Vietnam than ever before. The troop level had peaked at approximately 540,000. More than 100 Americans were returned in body bags every week.

Then, a battle brewing in the A Shau Valley in South Vietnam gave the antiwar movement even more ammunition. U.S. airmen were ordered to capture Dong Ap Bia. It was a hill that the communists were passing through to transport men and weapons to the coastal area around Hue. U.S. troops made several attempts to take the hill, only to be repelled by the North Vietnamese. They finally fought their way to the top, but 56 troops were killed and 421 more were wounded in the process.

Dong Ap Bia became known as Hamburger Hill because the fighting in this area "ground up" so many men. The thought of fighting there frightened and angered many U.S. soldiers. Many of them did not believe the dangerous mission was important enough to risk so many lives. U.S. soldier Patrick Power stated:

> *A lot of people felt it was [useless] going up time and time again. There was a lot of anger over that. Everyone knew after the first company went up that we'd be walking into ambushes each and every time.*[1]

The anger grew when Americans were ordered to withdraw from Dong Ap Bia less than a month after it had been taken. It was explained the need to hold it was gone since the enemy had been driven from the area. Many of those who had fought there and lost their friends did not accept that explanation. President Nixon and General Creighton Abrams also questioned the operation. They took steps to wind down the war by discontinuing further U.S. troop combat operations. The battle of Hamburger Hill marked the end of search-and-destroy tactics and the beginning of a more defensive war in an attempt to limit U.S. casualties.

Ho Chi Minh's Death

The end of an era in North Vietnam occurred on September 3, 1969, when Ho Chi Minh died of a heart attack. He had named Vietnamese Communist Party head Le Duan as his replacement. In his will, Minh urged his countrymen to continue the fight until the last American had left the country.

A New Policy

By that time, Nixon had already announced his intention to launch his "Vietnamization" program. This would shift the burden of fighting the NVA and Vietcong forces to the ARVN. Just as they did in the late 1950s and early 1960s, Americans would train and equip the South Vietnamese. In 1969, Nixon began slowly pulling U.S. combat troops out

Henry Kissinger

of Vietnam. He would continue to do so until they had all returned home by 1973.

The new policy had been carefully formed. National Security Advisor Henry Kissinger was committed to a negotiated peace. He believed it was the only way to avoid a communist takeover. But Nixon was not prepared to end U.S. involvement completely. A series of NVA attacks in South Vietnam in early 1969 prompted him to order heavy bombings of North Vietnamese base camps in Cambodia. Nixon correctly assumed that North

Vietnam would not protest because its leaders had denied they were operating in Cambodia.

Nixon kept the bombing secret from the public and even most government officials. He wanted to prevent further protests against the war. But despite the first withdrawals of U.S. troops and a peace plan Nixon announced on May 14, opposition to the war intensified.

Kissinger and North Vietnamese diplomat Xuan Thuy met in the summer of 1969 to discuss peace. Unfortunately, those talks were no more successful than previous ones. This prompted war hawks in the United States to call for a concentrated attack

Horror of Napalm

One of the most famous and gruesome photos taken during the war shows a badly burned nine-year-old girl named Kim Phuc. She is fleeing her village and screaming in pain after a napalm attack. Napalm is a gasoline mixture that was commonly used by Americans to burn forests, villages, and people. Reaching temperatures of 5,000 degrees Fahrenheit (2,760 degrees Celsius), it often burned people to the bone. Associated Press photographer Nick Ut, who won a Pulitzer Prize for his effort, took the picture of Kim Phuc racing naked in terror.

Ut poured water on the body of Kim Phuc and rushed her to the hospital, a heroic act that helped her survive. She eventually moved to Toronto, Canada, and on Veterans Day in 1996, she spoke to a crowd about her experience. She said:

As you know, I am the little girl who was running to escape from the napalm fire. I have suffered a lot from both physical and emotional pain. . . . We should try to do good things for the present and for the future to promote peace.[2]

on North Vietnam that included bombing strikes of both military and civilian targets. Nixon decided against such a bold move. Still, the antiwar movement gathered steam. In previous years, protests had been mostly organized. College students and peace activists attended them. But by 1969, millions of ordinary Americans had joined the protests.

On October 15, they participated in the first "Moratorium Day" to protest continued U.S. involvement in Vietnam. In large cities and small towns across the United States, church bells tolled, marchers holding candles read out the names of slain U.S. soldiers, and students staged timed walkouts from school. Similar demonstrations were held in England, France, and Australia. Even U.S. soldiers in Vietnam showed their antiwar solidarity by wearing black armbands on patrol.

Three weeks later, Nixon claimed an early withdrawal from Vietnam would result in a bloodbath and a loss of faith in U.S. leadership around the world. Both he and Vice President

Nixon's Secret

President Nixon's decision to keep the bombing of North Vietnam bases in Cambodia secret was just one event in a presidency marked by secrecy. He went on to cover up his own illegal activities in dealing with opponents of the war and his own political career in the early 1970s. The result was a scandal, referred to as Watergate, that in 1974 forced him to become the only president to resign from office.

"Silent Majority"

In pleading his case to the U.S. public, President Nixon called upon the "silent majority" to rise up and have their voices heard. Nixon considered those who supported the war to outnumber those who did not, though they did not express their views through protests and demonstrations.

Spiro Agnew criticized the antiwar protesters. Nixon claimed, "North Vietnam cannot defeat or humiliate the United States. Only Americans can do that."[3]

On November 15, an estimated 250,000 protesters converged on Washington DC on the second Moratorium Day. Many carried signs bearing the names of U.S. soldiers who had been killed in Vietnam. Similar demonstrations were held across the country.

By early 1970, however, it appeared that Nixon's Vietnamization program was beginning to work. The South Vietnamese army's performance in the field was improving. But U.S. military officials had been complaining for quite a while about the escape route the NVA and Vietcong used in Cambodia. The enemy also used the route to regroup and resupply. In late April, Nixon announced an invasion of Cambodia.

Soon six more Americans would be dead, but not in Vietnam or Cambodia. Their blood would be shed on the campuses of two U.S. universities.

Protesters paraded near the Capitol building as part of the second Moratorium Day on November 15, 1969.

The incident at Kent State left four students dead and nine injured.

TRAGEDY, BUT
NO TRIUMPH

A mericans gathered around their television sets on the night of April 30, 1970. They watched and listened as President Nixon announced that he was sending troops into Cambodia. The NVA and Vietcong had received sanctuary in Cambodia throughout the war. Nixon said that he was not about to sit idly by while the American people suffered the only military defeat in their history. Nixon's message was not what millions were hoping to hear. The reaction was violent on college campuses. Hundreds of student protests erupted over the expansion of the conflict.

COLLEGE CAMPUS SHOOTINGS

The antiwar movement at Kent State University in northeast Ohio had been relatively quiet. But Nixon's announcement motivated its students to take action. On May 2, they burned the Reserve Officers' Training Corps (ROTC) building to the ground and continued their demonstrations.

Ohio Governor James Rhodes called in National Guardsmen, who tried in vain to suppress the protest. Then on May 4, disaster struck. During a rally, frustrated National Guardsmen kneeled down, aimed their weapons, and shot into the crowd. By the time the bullets stopped firing, four Kent State students lay dead and nine others

Withdrawing Troops

In early 1970, U.S. senators drafted resolutions that would require U.S. troops to be withdrawn from Cambodia by June 30 and from Vietnam entirely by the end of 1971. The initiatives failed to pass, largely because Nixon removed the troops from Cambodia before June 30.

were wounded. A week later, two more students
at Jackson State College in Mississippi were killed
during a confrontation with police.

The reaction throughout the country to
the killings on college campuses was furious.
Demonstrations followed at dozens of schools.
Hundreds of thousands of students staged a strike
by refusing to attend classes, causing hundreds of
universities to shut
down by
mid-May.

Meanwhile, a
combined force of
15,000 U.S. and
South Vietnamese
soldiers plunged
into Cambodia
and found no
enemy. The North
Vietnamese had
fled. A base camp
with stockpiles
of weapons and
ammunition was
destroyed. This

An Early Morning Chat

Around 4:00 a.m. on May 10, 1970, six days
after the shootings at Kent State, a few students
from an antiwar protest were milling around
the Lincoln Memorial when President Nixon
suddenly showed up. Nixon, who had been
upset by the tragedy at Kent State and resulting
violence on college campuses, was restless. He
awakened his valet Manolo Sanchez and asked
him if he had ever seen the Lincoln Memorial
at night. Sanchez answered that he had not, so
Nixon invited him to accompany him there.

The president came upon the group of
students. One student, who attended the University of Syracuse, later described the rather
surreal experience to a reporter:

*I hope it was because he was tired, but
most of what [Nixon] was saying was
absurd. Here we had come from a university that's completely uptight, on strike,
and when we told him where we were
from, he talked about the football team.*[1]

temporarily relieved the threat to Saigon and other nearby spots in South Vietnam.

The political backlash to the invasion of Cambodia and campus shootings shook the White House. The Senate overwhelmingly voted to rescind the Gulf of Tonkin Resolution. It had become obvious that the tide of both public and political opinion had turned against U.S. involvement in Vietnam. And neither victory nor what Nixon perceived as an "honorable peace" was in sight.

The Beginning of the End

The U.S. priority following the Cambodian incursion was bringing soldiers home and turning the war effort over to the South Vietnamese. The priority of the North Vietnamese was to bide their time. They did little fighting, particularly in 1971, as they waited until only the South Vietnamese remained as an adversary.

The fate of South Vietnam was about to be entrusted to the South Vietnamese. Americans forged an officers training program to find military leaders in that country. Americans provided the most modern weaponry. And they allowed the South Vietnamese to accompany them on missions.

By 1971, the South Vietnamese boasted a million-man army and a capable air force and navy.

When the concept of Vietnamization was tested, though, the results were disastrous. Early in 1971, the ARVN spearheaded an attack into the nearby country of Laos. Like Cambodia, Laos was suspected of supplying and giving shelter to the communists. The approximately 21,000-man ARVN force established bases with no resistance. But it collapsed upon the weight of enemy fire. The ARVN retreated toward the South Vietnamese border under chase by the NVA. The retreat became disorganized and deteriorated despite help from the air by U.S. planes. Approximately 9,000 South Vietnamese were killed, wounded, or captured. More would have perished had not U.S. helicopter crews risked their lives to rescue them.

It was obvious the ARVN was not ready to take over the defense of its own country. However, the United States no longer had the force in Vietnam to do the job. By the end of 1971, fewer than 200,000 U.S. soldiers remained in Vietnam. And

John Wayne and Jane Fonda

During the course of the war, dozens of entertainers expressed their views on U.S. policy. Two of the most famous were actors John Wayne and Jane Fonda. Wayne was a staunch advocate of continued involvement in Vietnam and a strong supporter of Richard Nixon. Fonda was a vocal critic of both Lyndon Johnson and Nixon.

In 1971, the United States prepared the South Vietnamese to take over all military operations.

on March 29, 1973, the last American combat troops would leave the country.

The Veterans Protest

By that time, the antiwar movement had quieted down. The Vietnam Veterans Against the War staged the most significant protest in 1971. Thousands of soldiers who had returned home angry about what they considered to be a needless loss of life marched in Washington DC that April. Some ceremoniously discarded the medals they earned in Vietnam onto the steps of the Capitol.

Among the veterans who turned against the war was future presidential candidate John Kerry. He spoke to members of the Senate as part of the protest. He reprimanded Vice President Agnew, who had called antiwar protesters "misfits" in 1970. Kerry said:

> *In our opinion, and from our experience, there is nothing in South Vietnam which could happen that realistically threatens the United States of America. And to attempt to justify the loss of one American life in Vietnam, Cambodia, or Laos by linking such loss to the preservation of freedom, which those misfits supposedly abuse, is to us the height of criminal [deception]. It is that kind of [deception] which we feel has torn this country apart.*[2]

The effects of the Vietnam War would be felt for decades. But first, the final chapter of a long, painful story had to play out. ⌐

Daniel Ellsberg

One incident that shook the nation had to do with former U.S. Defense Department analyst Daniel Ellsberg. Ellsberg provided the *New York Times* with a copy of the Defense Department's secret history and analysis of the Vietnam War. The documents showed that President Johnson lied to the public about the progress of the war.

The administration attempted to prevent the newspaper from publishing what became known as the "Pentagon Papers." But the Supreme Court ruled that the *New York Times* had a legal right to publish the damaging documents, which it did in 1971.

Vietnam War veterans protested at the Capitol in 1971.

South Vietnamese troops were aided by U.S. air strikes.

HOLDING ON

In the spring of 1972, an estimated 40,000 North Vietnamese troops rolled toward the South Vietnamese provincial capital of Quang Tri City. Two weeks later, they had created two more fronts that sent the ARVN in a hasty retreat. By mid-April the collapse of South Vietnam appeared quite possible.

President Nixon was not about to call again for U.S. combat troops, but he still considered a communist takeover unacceptable. He hurriedly sent U.S. warships, aircraft carriers, warplanes, and 70,000 U.S. Air Force personnel into action. These forces blasted away at enemy supply lines. They also delivered a massive amount of equipment to the crippled ARVN, which had lost an estimated 30,000 men during the NVA offensive. Nixon ordered the resumption of bombing strikes against North Vietnam, a strategy he continued for the duration of the war.

U.S. bombers pounded dozens of military and industrial targets, many of them within just a few miles of the capital city of Hanoi. The president also authorized the mining of Haiphong Harbor in North Vietnam. This entailed dropping explosive devices in the water that would explode when ships sailed past them. That crippled the NVA's ability to resupply and played a role in saving South Vietnam— at least for the time being.

Peace Talks

Nixon and Kissinger understood, however, that the ARVN was likely incapable of halting the communist onslaught for much longer. They needed to give the North Vietnamese a reason to negotiate for peace. They achieved that objective when Nixon visited their allies in China and the Soviet Union. It has been speculated that the diplomatic missions frightened the North Vietnamese into believing that those nations might withdraw military support.

Peace talks resumed in Paris between Kissinger and North Vietnamese negotiator Le Duc Tho. Finally in October 1972, it appeared an agreement had been reached. The United States dropped its

Nurses

Though only men participated in combat, women also played a part in the U.S. role in the Vietnam War. About 8,000 of the 9,000 women in the military were nurses, and eight U.S. nurses died in Vietnam.

One nurse, Lily Lee Adams, worked at an evacuation hospital for one year starting in October 1969. Adams and her fellow nurses gained tremendous respect from the soldiers they treated. She told one story that was particularly meaningful to her:

There was this infantry captain who came through. He says to me, "Ma'am, I have all the respect in the world for you." I say, "What for?" He says, "Ma'am, I couldn't do what you are doing. I'd rather be out in the [field] ducking the [enemy] than be in here doing your job." I heard that over and over in Vietnam. I didn't have to ask for respect over there—I got it.[1]

demand that the NVA leave South
Vietnam. Despite objections from
the South Vietnamese government,
Kissinger announced in late October
that peace was at hand. The timing
could not have been better for
Nixon, particularly because the
presidential election was merely a
week away. He defeated Democratic
candidate George McGovern easily to
earn a second term.

No Peace Yet

The proclamation that peace
was about to take hold in Vietnam
was, however, quite premature.
The Paris peace talks collapsed in
mid-December when the United
States renewed its request that
the NVA withdraw from South
Vietnam. North Vietnam refused
to compromise. The angered
Nixon responded by initiating the
war's heaviest bombing campaign
yet. An estimated 400,000 tons

**China and
the Soviet Union**

One reason Nixon felt it
necessary to pull U.S. soldiers out of Vietnam was
that he hoped to create
better relationships with
communist powers China
and the Soviet Union. In
February 1972, Nixon
became the first president
ever to visit China since
it had become a com-
munist country. In July, he
also signed an agreement
with Soviet leader Leonid
Brezhnev that limited
weapons production in
both countries.

Henry Kissinger, right, met with North Vietnamese delegate Le Duc Tho, left, during the peace talks that resulted in the Paris Peace Accords.

(362,878 tonnes) of bombs rained down on Hanoi and Haiphong. Despite worldwide criticism of the bombing, it had its desired effect. The North Vietnamese were again negotiating for peace by the end of the year.

This time, the talks made progress. Desperate to reach an agreement, the United States again agreed to allow the NVA to remain in South Vietnam despite heated objections from the South Vietnamese leaders. The U.S. government stipulated that the South Vietnamese had to agree to the terms if it hoped to continue receiving American aid. Representatives from the United States, South Vietnam, North Vietnam, and the Vietcong signed the Paris Peace Accords on January 27, 1973. The document stated that all parties must immediately halt military action in South Vietnam.

Vietnam would have two governments—one led by current, as of 1967, President Thieu and the other controlled by the communists. The peace accords also stated that the reunification of Vietnam must proceed peacefully. But in a country that had been torn by war for more than a half century, that was not likely to happen.

Indeed, the fighting was not over. Nixon suspected that the NVA

Henry Kissinger

Henry Kissinger is considered one of the foremost experts on foreign relations in U.S. history. Kissinger remained the nation's national security adviser after negotiating the Paris Peace Accords that ended U.S. involvement in Vietnam. But he also took over as U.S. secretary of state in September 1973 and stayed at the post for four years. He remained an important adviser to U.S. presidents well into his eighties.

would attempt to unify the nation by force. He wrote a letter to Thieu vowing that the United States would take swift military action if the North Vietnamese broke the conditions of the peace agreement. And because the Paris accords applied only to Vietnam, U.S. warplanes continued to bomb NVA supply routes in Cambodia. But that threat would never be delivered. Later that year, the War Powers Act was passed. It mandated Congressional approval before a president could send troops to war.

Americans and their political leaders were tired of the war. Many believed that the peace treaty would hold up and keep the North Vietnamese and Vietcong from renewing military action. They believed wrong. An unhappy ending to the long drama was about to unfold. ⌐

Prisoners of War

Many U.S. soldiers were taken prisoner by the North Vietnamese and were held captive for years during the war. Some of them were tortured. Part of the peace agreement reached in Paris stated that these prisoners be returned. By early April 1973, all 591 prisoners of war had been returned to the United States.

By the last stages of the war, most U.S. soldiers had returned home.

Vietnamese citizens climbed the walls of the U.S. Embassy in Saigon on April 29, 1975. They were attempting to reach evacuation helicopters.

THE END
AND AFTERMATH

The guns and artillery were supposed to fall silent in Vietnam on January 28, 1973, but they did not. The cease-fire was to be overseen by the International Commission of Control and Support (ICCS), which consisted of representatives from Poland, Hungary, Canada, and Indonesia. But neither the Paris Peace Accords nor the ICCS were given a chance to succeed by either side. Fighting between the ARVN and communist troops continued throughout South Vietnam.

Both sides renewed hostilities and claimed the other side had violated the peace accords. South Vietnamese President Thieu proved particularly unwilling to observe the treaty. Clark Dougan and Stephen Weiss, authors of a ten-volume series on the war, wrote:

> *Thieu acted from the outset as if the accords didn't exist. Still wedded to the "four no's" he had first proclaimed in 1969— no negotiating with the enemy, no communist activity in South Vietnam, no surrender of territory, no coalition government— he [ruined] any possibility of a political solution.[1]*

Thieu ordered the ARVN to strike NVA military bases and communist-controlled villages in various areas of South Vietnam. The result was more carnage as 6,000 South Vietnamese soldiers lost their lives during the first three months of what was intended to be peace.

Despite the broken promises on both sides, Nixon secretly continued to supply South Vietnam with weapons and equipment. He also promised full military and economic aid if the North Vietnamese attempted a takeover. But North Vietnam assumed mostly a defensive posture during the first year of the cease-fire. Nixon was hindered in November 1973 when a vote in Congress required him to give two full days' notice to both the House of Representatives and the Senate for deployment of U.S. troops to South Vietnam. It further ordered that those troops would have to leave the country within two months unless Congress approved their continued presence. By August 1974, Nixon had resigned from office in disgrace after attempting to hush up many illegal activities committed by his staff.

Undaunted, Thieu ordered his forces to launch ground and air attacks on NVA bases and communist strongholds. The unprepared NVA suffered heavy losses but recovered

Unpopular Wars

The Vietnam War proved unpopular among the American people. By the end of the war, far more than 50 percent of those polled wanted U.S. involvement in the war to end. But it was not the last war to gain such unpopularity. Several years later, Americans were polled about the Iraq War, which began in 2003. It showed a vast majority opposed to the war that began under President George W. Bush.

to counterattack in late spring 1974. The North Vietnamese regained all the land they had lost and seized additional territory.

It was the beginning of the end for Thieu and the ARVN. The North Vietnamese struck again in December. In early March 1975, they captured the city of Ban Me Thuot. Thieu ordered an evacuation of South Vietnamese forces. Both troops and civilians retreated. This led to disorganization and confusion. Then the North Vietnamese headed straight for the South Vietnamese capital of Saigon.

The Last Days of War

Both Hue and Da Nang, cities that the Americans and ARVN had been so desperate to hold earlier in the war, quickly fell to the communists. Trying to prevent the advance was useless. Many felt the communist takeover was merely a matter of time.

Volunteer Military

The draft sent many young men to Vietnam. But, as of 2009, the draft had not been used in any U.S. war since the Vietnam War. The United States used a strictly volunteer military from which it selected soldiers to fight in both the Gulf War and Iraq War.

On April 21, President Thieu resigned. He blamed the United States for the disaster and said, "The United States has not respected its promises. It is inhumane. It is untrustworthy. It is irresponsible."[2]

The U.S. government organized an airlift of approximately 2,000 South Vietnamese babies and young children, carrying them to safety in the United States and other countries. However, the first airplane crashed shortly after takeoff and resulted in dozens of deaths. But an estimated 1,300 others did survive the airlifts. Families in the

Welcome Home

When the thousands of U.S. soldiers returned home from World War II, they returned in groups and were greeted with hearty handshakes and parades. But when the U.S. soldiers returned home from Vietnam, usually arriving by themselves, they were greeted by empty airport terminals and even scorn. Many soldiers settled back into their regular routines and went on to live productive lives. But more than 100,000 soldiers returned with major physical or emotional problems. Some of those who were wounded in Vietnam were unable to work due to amputated limbs or paralysis. Others suffered severe emotional problems from their war experiences. Still others returned as drug addicts or alcoholics.

Many veterans are still filled with anger over the war and the treatment they received from their fellow Americans upon their return. One moment that began the healing process occurred on Veterans Day in 1982, when the Vietnam Veterans Memorial was unveiled in Washington DC. That day, 150,000 veterans gathered for its formal dedication. The memorial, in the design of a V-shaped wall, bears the names of all 58,260 Americans who died in the war.

United States and other countries adopted them.

The remaining Americans in Vietnam were also evacuated by helicopter shortly after a North Vietnamese attack near Saigon on April 29, 1975. Thousands of South Vietnamese begged to be evacuated by the Americans as well. Approximately 6,000 were brought onto crowded ships. Many parents brought their children to the ships, knowing they would never see them again. Thousands of other South Vietnamese escaped in their own boats.

General Duong Van Minh, who had replaced Thieu as head of the government, announced the surrender of South Vietnam the next day. North Vietnamese and Vietcong troops rolled into Saigon, which was renamed Ho Chi Minh City. Vietnam was united under a communist flag.

The Domino Theory

Those who used the domino theory as an argument in favor of U.S. involvement in Vietnam in the early 1960s had no further arguments after the war. Though South Vietnam, Laos, and Cambodia did fall to communism, the same did not happen to any other countries in Southeast Asia as a direct or indirect result.

Vietnamese refugees crowded onto a military ship during evacuation.

Peace in the United States

Americans also had obtained peace. But the divisions caused by the Vietnam War continued to separate the nation. It also raised questions about foreign policy and how Americans treat their fellow citizens. Even today, those who supported U.S. involvement in Vietnam argue that the antiwar movement prevented the nation's leaders from taking all steps necessary to win. They believe that those who marched and protested did a disservice to the entire war effort.

Those against the war believe that the more than 58,000 U.S. men killed in Vietnam died in vain. Intervening in a civil war thousands of miles away was morally wrong, they say. They contend that by protesting, they were exercising their rights as Americans and supporting the troops in Vietnam by trying to bring them home.

The arguments over such issues continue to rage. However, there can be little doubt that the experience in Vietnam changed the relationship between the U.S. government and its people. Americans have become far more likely to question their leaders, not just about war but about all issues concerning the country.

Many of the emotional wounds have healed since the North

Disappointment

Many former Vietcong who found a place in the Vietnamese government after the war expressed severe disappointment with the North Vietnamese communists. Among them was Truong Nhu Tang, who served as minister of justice until 1976. Tang said, "With total power in their hands, they began to show their cards in the most brutal fashion."[3]

Though still a communist country, Vietnam instituted social and economic changes in the 1980s that spurred growth. The standard of living has improved dramatically. Vietnam has since forged diplomatic ties with many Western countries, including the United States. Presidents Bill Clinton and George W. Bush both made official visits to Vietnam.

Vietnamese and Vietcong secured the only wartime defeat in U.S. history. But the legacy of the Vietnam War has remained—how it divided, angered, and frustrated the American people and their leaders. At the same time, the Vietnam era was one of learning and understanding for all Americans. ⌐

The Vietnam War Memorial

TIMELINE

1950	1955	1961
U.S. military involvement in Vietnam begins as President Truman authorizes aid to the French on July 26.	In January, the first direct shipment of U.S. military aid to Saigon arrives.	On October 24, helicopter units become the first Americans involved in combat operations.

1965	1965	1967
On July 28, President Johnson announces he will increase the U.S. military presence in Vietnam to 125,000 men.	The Battle of Ia Drang Valley between U.S. troops and the NVA in South Vietnam occurs in November.	From January 8 to 26, Operation Cedar Falls uncovers an extensive network of tunnels used by the Vietcong.

1964

On August 2, three North Vietnamese patrol boats attack the USS *Maddox* in the Gulf of Tonkin.

1964

On August 7, the Gulf of Tonkin Resolution grants power to President Johnson to wage an undeclared war in Vietnam.

1965

Operation Rolling Thunder begins on February 24.

1967

In July, General Westmoreland requests an additional 200,000 troops. President Johnson agrees to 45,000.

1967

From October 21 to October 23, demonstrations at the Pentagon draw 50,000 protesters and become violent.

1968

The 77-day NVA siege of the U.S. air base at Khe Sanh begins on January 21.

TIMELINE

1968	**1968**	**1968**
On January 30, the Tet Offensive results in a victory for the United States.	On March 16, U.S. soldiers kill more than 500 men, women, and children in the South Vietnamese village of My Lai.	President Johnson drops out of the presidential race on March 31.

1970	**1972**	**1973**
At Kent State University in Ohio, National Guardsmen kill four student protesters on May 4.	On May 8, Nixon announces the mining of North Vietnam's harbors and intensified bombing.	The Paris Peace Accords are signed on January 27.

1968

On August 28, during the Democratic National Convention in Chicago, 10,000 antiwar protesters gather on downtown streets.

1969

President Nixon announces the "Vietnamization" plan on June 8.

1970

On April 30, President Nixon announces a U.S. and South Vietnamese incursion into Cambodia.

1973

On March 29, the last remaining U.S. combat troops withdraw from Vietnam.

1975

On March 10, the final offensive begins as 25,000 NVA troops attack Ban Me Thuot.

1975

On April 30, the last Americans depart Saigon. The North Vietnamese complete the takeover, ending the war.

Essential Facts

Date of Event

1950–1975

Place of Event

South Vietnam, North Vietnam, Cambodia, Laos, United States

Key Players

- ❖ Ho Chi Minh, North Vietnamese leader
- ❖ Ngo Dinh Diem, president of South Vietnam until assassination in 1963
- ❖ North Vietnamese Army (NVA)
- ❖ Vietcong
- ❖ National Liberation Front (NLF)
- ❖ South Vietnamese Army (ARVN)
- ❖ President John F. Kennedy
- ❖ President Lyndon Johnson
- ❖ General William Westmoreland, commander of U.S. forces in Vietnam from 1964 to 1968
- ❖ President Richard Nixon
- ❖ Nguyen Van Thieu, president of South Vietnam from 1967 to 1975

HIGHLIGHTS OF EVENT

❖ North Vietnam and the Vietcong took military action in South Vietnam in the 1950s and 1960s to unify the country under a communist government.

❖ United States sent aid to help South Vietnam stave off assault. More than 2 million U.S. troops were used to try to prevent communist North Vietnam from taking over South Vietnam.

❖ The U.S. antiwar movement called for an end to U.S. involvement in Vietnam.

❖ The North Vietnamese and Vietcong completed a military victory in 1975, unifying all of Vietnam under communist rule.

QUOTE

"Among my sergeants, there were men who had parachuted into Normandy [during the invasion of Europe in World War II] and had survived the war in Korea—and those old veterans were shocked by the savagery and hellish noise of this battle. Choking clouds of smoke and dust obscured the killing ground. We were dry-mouthed and [overcome] with fear, and still the enemy came on in waves."
—Hal Moore, Vietnam War battalion commander

ADDITIONAL RESOURCES

SELECT BIBLIOGRAPHY

Dougan, Clark, and Stephen Weiss. *The American Experience in Vietnam*. Boston, MA: Boston Publishing Company, 1988.

Edmonds, Anthony O. *The War in Vietnam*. Westport, CT: Greenwood Press, 1998.

Franklin, Jane, H. Bruce Franklin, Marvin Gettleman, and Marilyn Young. *Vietnam and America*. New York, NY: Grove Press, 1995.

Schell, Jonathan. *The Real War: The Classic Reporting on the Vietnam War*. New York, NY: Pantheon Books, 1987.

FURTHER READING

Fitzgerald, Brian. *Fighting the Vietnam War*. Chicago, IL: Raintree, 2006.

Wiest, Andrew. *The Vietnam War, 1964–1975*. New York, NY: Osprey Publishing, 2002.

Yamasaki, Mitch. *Vietnam War: How the United States Became Involved*. Topeka, KS: Topeka Bindery, 2001.

Web Links

To learn more about U.S. involvement in Vietnam, visit ABDO Publishing Company online at **www.abdopublishing.com**. Web sites about U.S. involvement in Vietnam are featured on our Book Links page. These links are routinely monitored and updated to provide the most current information available.

Places to Visit

National Vietnam War Museum
3400 North Tanner Road, Orlando, FL 32826
407-601-2864
www.nwmvocf.org
The museum holds many artifacts of the Vietnam War. Many of the artifacts have been donated by the Vietnam Veterans of Central Florida.

The Vietnam Center and Archive, Texas Tech University
Eighteenth and Boston Avenue, Lubbock, TX 79409
806-742-9010
www.vietnam.ttu.edu
The Vietnam Center and Archive at Texas Tech University supports research and education focused on the Vietnam experience.

Vietnam Veterans Memorial
900 Ohio Drive Southwest, Washington, DC 20242
202-426-6841 or 202-619-7225
thewall-usa.com
The V-shaped wall lists the names of more than 58,000 Americans who were killed during the Vietnam War.

GLOSSARY

ARVN

The Army of the Republic of Vietnam that fought for the South Vietnamese during the war.

base

A protected centralized location from which military operations are planned and begin.

Buddhist

An individual who practices Buddhism, a religion most prevalent in Asia.

capitalism

An economic system in which the means of production are privately owned and it is governed by the principles of a free-market economy: supply and demand.

communism

An economic and political system in which the government, or state, controls the economy.

demonstration

A large public gathering of people who come together to express their views on a particular issue or cause.

domino theory

The belief of some following World War II that the loss of one country to communism would result in the falling of others one by one.

draft

The process by which American men were selected and legally required to fight in Vietnam.

military advisers

U.S. noncombatants who trained and advised South Vietnamese military personnel before, during, and after U.S. involvement in the Vietnam War.

NLF

National Liberation Front. An antigovernment organization in South Vietnam that called for an end to U.S. involvement in Vietnam and the reunification of the country.

offensive

> A major military attack carried out by a large number of soldiers for the purpose of capturing territory or otherwise helping the war effort.

overthrow

> The usually violent act of pushing a political leader or political leaders out of power in a particular country.

poll

> A sampling of opinions on a subject taken from a group of people.

sanctuary

> A safe haven.

siege

> The military blockade of a fort or base with the intention of forcing surrender.

veteran

> Any soldier who returns from fighting in a war.

Vietcong

> A group of communist soldiers from South Vietnam who sympathized and fought with the North Vietnamese during the war.

Vietminh

> The original military force and government of North Vietnam led by Ho Chi Minh.

Vietnamization

> President Nixon's plan beginning in 1969 to transfer military responsibilities from the Americans to the South Vietnamese.

SOURCE NOTES

Chapter 1. Holiday Surprise

1. Clark Dougan and Stephen Weiss. *The American Experience in Vietnam*. Boston: Boston Publishing Company, 1988. 146.
2. Anthony O. Edmonds. *The War in Vietnam*. Westport, CT: Greenwood Press, 1998. 59.
3. Clark Dougan and Stephen Weiss. *The American Experience in Vietnam*. Boston: Boston Publishing Company, 1988. 149.
4. Jonathan Schell. *The Real War: The Classic Reporting on the Vietnam War*. New York: Pantheon Books, 1987. 37.
5. Anthony O. Edmonds. *The War in Vietnam*. Westport, CT: Greenwood Press, 1998. 61.

Chapter 2. War on the Horizon
None.

Chapter 3. The Green Light

1. Clark Dougan and Stephen Weiss. *The American Experience in Vietnam*. Boston: Boston Publishing Company, 1988. 28.
2. "Transcript—LBJ Goes to War." *The American Experience: Vietnam Online*. PBS Online. 1997. 14 Jan. 2009 <http://www.pbs.org/wgbh/amex/vietnam/104ts.html>.
3. John F. Kennedy Presidential Library and Museum. "JFK in History: The Cold War." 15 Jan. 2009 <http://www.jfklibrary.org/Historical+Resources/JFK+in+History/The+Cold+War+Page+2.htm>.
4. Clark Dougan and Stephen Weiss. *The American Experience in Vietnam*. Boston: Boston Publishing Company, 1988. 57.
5. Anthony O. Edmonds. *The War in Vietnam*. Westport, CT: Greenwood Press, 1998. 54.

Chapter 4. Getting in Deeper and Deeper

1. "Defeat American Escalation: Report to the National Assembly of the Democratic Republic of Vietnam (1965)." Excerpt from Ho Chi Minh Address. *Vietnam Courier*. 15 Apr. 1965.

Chapter 5. Conflict on the Home Front

1. Jeff Leen. "The Vietnam Protests: When Worlds Collide." *Washington Post*. 27 Sept. 1999. A1.
2. Clark Dougan, and Stephen Weiss. *The American Experience in Vietnam*. Boston: Boston Publishing Company, 1988. 114–115.
3. Ibid. 116.
4. Marvin Gettleman, Jane Franklin, Marilyn Young, and H. Bruce Franklin. *Vietnam and America*. New York: Grove Press, 1995. 339.

Chapter 6. The World Is Watching

1. Clark Dougan and Stephen Weiss. *The American Experience in Vietnam*. Boston: Boston Publishing Company, 1988. 208.

Chapter 7. Inching Out

1. Debbie Levy. *The Vietnam War*. Minneapolis: Lerner Publications, 2004. 52.
2. Michael Taylor. "Incineration: Military Says Goodbye to Napalm." *San Francisco Chronicle*. mindfully.org. 4 April 2001. 19 Jan. 2009 <http://www.mindfully.org/Plastic/Napalm-Recycled.htm>.
3. Clark Dougan and Stephen Weiss. *The American Experience in Vietnam*. Boston: Boston Publishing Company, 1988. 242.

Chapter 8. Tragedy, but No Triumph

1. Anthony O. Edmonds. *The War in Vietnam*. Westport, CT: Greenwood Press, 1998. 71.
2. John Kerry. "Testimony before the Senate Foreign Relations Committee." 22 Apr. 1971. *Congressional Record*, Vol. 117:57.

SOURCE NOTES CONTINUED

Chapter 9. Holding On
1. Kathryn Marshall. "Lily Lee Adams." *In the Combat Zone*.
New York: Penguin Books, 1988. 206–229.

Chapter 10. The End and Aftermath
1. Clark Dougan and Stephen Weiss. *The American Experience in Vietnam*.
Boston: Boston Publishing Company, 1988. 307.
2. Malcolm W. Browne. "Theiu Resigns, Calls U.S.
Untrustworthy." *New York Times*. 22 Apr. 1975. A1.
3. Truong Nhu Tang. *A Viet Cong Memoir: An Inside Account of the Vietnam
War and Its Aftermath*. New York: Vintage Books, 1985. 6.

INDEX

Index Continued

ABOUT THE AUTHOR

Martin Gitlin is a freelance writer based in northeast Ohio.
He won more than 40 awards as a newspaper reporter, including
first place for general excellence from Associated Press in 1995.
That organization also selected him as one of the top four feature
writers in the state in 2001. Gitlin has written more than a dozen
educational books, including books in the Essential Events series
on *Brown v. the Board of Education*, *The Battle of the Little Bighorn*, *The 1929
Stock Market Crash*, and *Operation Desert Storm*.

PHOTO CREDITS

AP Images, cover, 15, 16, 20, 26, 30, 35, 40, 44, 47, 54, 58, 61,
65, 69, 70, 77, 78, 92, 96 (bottom), 97, 98, 99 (top); Nick Ut/
AP Images, 6; Johner/AP Images, 9, 96 (top); Red Line Editorial,
25; Bill Ingraham/AP Images, 36; Horst Faas/AP Images, 43;
Peter Arnett/AP Images, 53; Hubert Van Es/AP Images, 62; Henri
Huet/AP Images, 75; Michel Lipchitz/AP Images, 82; Sal Veder/
AP Images, 85, 99 (bottom, left); Neal Ulevich/AP Images, 86, 99
(bottom, right); Mark Wilson/Getty Images, 95